"FIGURING" MODERN SPORT: AUTOBIOGRAPHICAL AND HISTORICAL REFLECTIONS ON SPORT, VIOLENCE AND CIVILISATION

Eric Dunning

Visiting Professor of Sociology of Sport

Emeritus Professor of Sociology,
University of Leicester
Visiting Professor of Sociology of Sport,
University College Dublin

An Inaugural Lecture
Delivered at University College Chester
on 28 October 2004

Chester Academic Press

First published 2005
by Chester Academic Press
Learning Resources
University College Chester
Parkgate Road
Chester CH1 4BJ

Printed and bound in the UK by the
Learning Resources Print Unit,
University College Chester
Cover designed by the
Learning Resources Graphics Team
University College Chester

©Eric Dunning, 2005

All Rights Reserved
No part of this publication may be reproduced, stored in a
retrieval system or transmitted in any form or by any
means without the prior permission of the copyright
owner, other than as permitted by current UK legislation
or under the terms of a recognised copyright licensing
scheme

A catalogue record for this publication is available from
the British Library

"FIGURING" MODERN SPORT: AUTOBIOGRAPHICAL AND HISTORICAL REFLECTIONS ON SPORT, VIOLENCE AND CIVILISATION

Good evening, ladies and gentlemen. I consider it a great honour to have been asked to give this inaugural lecture at the Centre for Research into Sport and Society — the CCRSS — here at University College Chester. I hope that all of us connected with the CCRSS will be able to make useful and important contributions to this exciting new stage in the history of UCC.

Mention of the CCRSS makes me think that a better title for my lecture might have been: "From Leicester to Chester: Medieval Hooligans on the Rood Dee and Their Counterparts Today". That, at least, gives you a clue as to what will be a central part of my subject-matter this evening: the development of football and football hooliganism. However, what I plan in a deeper sense to do is to examine the "figuring" of modern sport in two senses of the term:

1. How people have *configured* themselves — the patterns they have formed — in the competitive psycho-physical leisure activities that have been called "sport" since the eighteenth century; and

2. How sociologists and others have "figured out", that is, contributed to the *understanding* or *explanation* of how and why such changes have occurred and are continuing to do so in the social field of sport . I shall concentrate, as I have through most of my career, on football.

The sociologists among you will have recognized that I am hinting, through the term "figuring", at the "figurational" or "process-sociological" approach pioneered by the late Norbert Elias. Elias is now

1

"Figuring" Modern Sport

increasingly becoming recognized as having been one of the greatest sociologists of the twentieth century, partly for his pioneering work in the sociology of sport. The fact that he was a major early contributor to this field is connected with his denial of the idea that "physical" phenomena are of lower value than "intellectual" phenomena: he saw them as interwoven and equal. He also argued that understanding movement and emotions is as important for a full understanding of humans as understanding thought and rationality. In fact, he denied the separate existence of "body" and "mind", arguing that sociology should be concerned with every aspect of humans and their social lives. Let me say a word or two about sociology generally.

Probably one of the most notable features of sociology is that it has tended over the years to be *discontinuous* as a subject, with new generations frequently rebelling against the approaches of their teachers. One of the many negative consequences of this is that we have been forced repeatedly to "reinvent the wheel", with practitioners who think they are being original repeating what their predecessors have done, without apparently being aware of that fact. Two examples of this which come readily to mind are Durkheim's (1893/1964) anticipation of core features of the "labelling theory of deviance" and Elias's anticipation of most of the features of post-structuralism and postmodernism that are of lasting value.

But let me return to the theme of discontinuity. One of its further consequences is difficulties of communication between the generations, but we figurational sociologists of sport have arguably managed to buck the trend and to achieve a degree of inter-generational continuity that is perhaps only surpassed by that achieved by Marxists. In a book co-edited by Joe Maguire and Kevin Young and published in 2002, I suggested in my chapter that there

"Figuring" Modern Sport

have so far been five generations of figurational sociologists of sport in the United Kingdom, namely:

1. Norbert Elias;
2. Me;
3. Pat Murphy, Ken Sheard and Ivan Waddington[1];
4. Joe Maguire and Grant Jarvie; and
5. Sharon Colwell, Graham Curry, Dominic Malcolm, Louise Mansfield, Martin Roderick and Stuart Smith.

The chapter in which I made this point was published in 2002, but written in 2001. Since then, a sixth generation of figurational sociologists of sport has started to mature. I am referring, of course, to Ken Green, Daniel Bloyce, Katie Liston and Andy Smith, a quartet who, I am sure, are certain to become known soon as "the Chester School" and who will hopefully take up the baton from the senescent "Leicester School" and push the understanding of sporting figurations further than we oldies managed to achieve.

What are the core features of the approach to sociology shared by these six generations of figurational sociologists of sport?[2] In the context of the present lecture, there is only time for me to list these core features abstractly and briefly. They are:

1. The shared conviction that, like the universe at large, human individuals and the societies they form are processes;
2. The idea that the processes undergone by societies have tended up to now, especially in the longer

---

[1] I should like to take this opportunity to express my heartfelt thanks to Pat Murphy, Ken Sheard and Ivan Waddington. Over the years that we have worked together, they have helped me in numerous ways and not just academically. I am very grateful to them all.
[2] Elias set forth his distinctive views on sociology at greatest length in *What is Sociology?* (1978).

"Figuring" Modern Sport

term, to be "blind", in the sense of being the largely unintended consequences of aggregates of intended individual acts. Elias sometimes used the metaphor of history as a runaway express train in order to illustrate this point. It was his hope that sociological knowledge will help us to bring the "train" of history under greater conscious control. He was fully aware, of course, that his stress on relative lack of control runs counter to the self-love of people who like to believe that they are always on top of things, always in control;

3. The idea that human societies consist of individuals who are radically interdependent. That is, we are born as a result of an act by our interdependent parents into a structured collectivity or social world that we ourselves played no part in forming and that occupies a particular position in time and space;

4. That power is a universal property of human relations at all levels of social integration, ranging from two-person groups to humanity as a whole. Power, according to Elias, is:

    (a) A function of interdependency ties. Your power over me is largely a consequence of the degree of my dependency on you;

    (b) A question of balances or ratios; and

    (c) Not explainable solely by reference to single factors, such as ownership of the means of production or control of the means of violence[3].

---

[3] It is, of course, Marxists who explain social structure and social change reductively by reference to ownership of the means of production or "economic forces". Max Weber added control of the means of violence to the equation. However, Elias rejected both such "factor theorizing" and the idea that law-like explanations are adequate in relation to the

"Figuring" Modern Sport

Elias also took account of such bodily power resources of individuals as physical and intellectual strength and such structural power resources of collectivities as degrees of group unity and cohesion. Bodily power resources, are, of course, centrally relevant to the sociology of sport.

5. Elias stressed the need in sociology for a constant two-way traffic between theory and research. Theory without research, he argued, is liable to be abstract and meaningless; research without theory to be arid and descriptive.

6. Elias argued that sociologists should see as their primary concern the building-up of and adding to bodies of reliable knowledge. He was firmly against the intrusion of political, religious and other ideologies into sociological research and suggested that, in a piece of research into, for example, a subject such as football hooliganism, we should aim, first of all by means of what he called "a detour *via* detachment", to build up as "reality-congruent" a picture as possible of what football hooliganism actually involves and of how and why it is socially and psychologically generated. Then, through a process of what he called "secondary reinvolvement", we should use our more reality-congruent knowledge to devise a more realistic and effective policy for dealing with the problem than was previously applied.

7. And finally, for present purposes, a further shared conviction of the six generations of figurational sociologists of sport is that Elias's theory of

---

human-social level of reality. He favoured what he called "structure and process explanations".

"Figuring" Modern Sport

civilising processes is what he called a central theory through which a variety of apparently diverse and separate phenomena - e.g., sport (Elias & Dunning, 1986), food (Mennell, 1985) and fire (Goudsblom, 1992) - can be related. Let me briefly give you a flavour of what the theory of civilizing processes entails.

Contrary to a fairly widespread misconception, Elias did not use the concept of a "civilising process" in a moral or evaluative way. He also usually enclosed the term "civilization" and its derivatives in inverted commas in order to signal this. "Civilizing process" was, for him, a technical term. He did not suggest that people who can be shown to stand at a more advanced level in a civilizing process than some others, for example ourselves relative to the people of feudal Britain, are in any meaningful sense "better than" or "morally superior to" those medieval people. That, of course, is almost invariably how the people who call themselves "civilized" view themselves. But how, Elias used to ask, can people congratulate themselves when they are the chance beneficiaries of a blind process to the course of which they have not personally contributed? To say this, of course, is not to deny that, just as tends to be the case with social processes generally, there are victims as well as beneficiaries of "civilizing" processes.

The theory of civilizing processes is in equal parts theoretical and empirical. Empirically, it is based on a substantial body of data, principally on the changing manners of the secular upper classes - the knights, kings, queens, court aristocrats, politicians and business leaders, but not, for the most part, the higher clergy - between the Middle Ages and modern times. These data indicate that, in the societies of Western Europe - Elias's *central* focus was on France, Germany and England - a long-term

"Figuring" Modern Sport

"blind" or unintended process took place involving four principal inter-related components:

1. The elaboration and refinement of social standards;
2. An increase in the social pressure on people to exercise stricter, more continuous and more even self-control over their feelings and behaviour;
3. A shift in the balance between external constraints and self-constraints in favour of self-constraints;
4. An increase at the levels of personality and habitus in the importance of "conscience" or "superego" as a regulator of behaviour. That is, social standards came to be internalized more deeply and to operate, not simply consciously and with an element of choice, but also beneath the levels of rationality and conscious control.

An aspect of this overall process which is of central relevance for understanding the development of modern sport has been the increasing control of violence and aggression *within* societies, though not to anything like the same extent in the relations between them. According to Elias, this taming of aggression took place together with a long-term decline in most people's capacity for obtaining pleasure from inflicting pain on others and for directly witnessing seriously violent acts. He referred in this connection to a dampening of *Angriffslust* — literally, to a clamping down or curbing of the lust for attacking: that is, a taming of people's conscious desire to obtain pleasure from attacking others and seeing them suffer, together with a reduction at the levels of personality and habitus in their learned capacity for doing so. This was connected, according to Elias, with an increase in mutual identification; that is, in reciprocal sympathy and understanding.

The terms "violence" and "civilization" tend to be understood popularly as antitheses. However, the civilizing processes of Western Europe were seen by Elias as the unplanned outcomes of violent struggles for supremacy among monarchs and other feudal lords. These struggles led to the establishment within the emergent European nation states - at different times and in somewhat differing ways - of relatively stable and effective state monopolies on violence and taxation, the major means of ruling in societies above the level of tribes. Modern nation states were formed to a large extent for purposes of war, but their violence and tax monopolies helped their central rulers not only in relation to external attack and defence, but also with regard to internal pacification. As they became internally more pacified, so the personality and habitus structure of the majority of their people became more peaceful and, as we shall see, this was reflected in what they began around the eighteenth century to call their "sports". The evidence suggests that this development in terminology, habitus and leisure institutions began to take place first of all in England.

Summing up, and at the risk of some oversimplification, one could express Elias's theory by saying that he held a civilizing process basically to be a consequence of five interdependent and interacting part-processes. These are:

1. State-formation;
2. Pacification under state-control;
3. Growing social differentiation and the lengthening of interdependency chains;
4. Growing equality of power chances between social classes, men and women, and the older and younger generations;

"Figuring" Modern Sport

5. Growing wealth[4].

Elias also showed how, in the course of a civilizing process, overtly violent struggles tend to be transformed into relatively peaceful struggles for status, wealth and power in which, in the most frequent course of events, destructive urges come to be kept for the most part beneath the threshold of consciousness and not translated into overt action. As we shall see, status struggles of this kind appear to have played an important part in the split between the soccer and rugby forms of football. This is an appropriate point at which to start examining figurational contributions to the sociological study of sport.

Figurational Contributions to the Sociological Study of Sport

Figurational studies in the sociology of sport have so far been mainly concerned with nine problem areas: namely, the development of modern sport in the context of European civilizing processes (Elias & Dunning, 1986; Dunning, 1999); the growing socio-cultural centrality of sport and its correlative commercialization, professionalization and monetarization (Dunning & Sheard, 1979/2005); football hooliganism, and spectator and player violence in sport more generally (Dunning, Murphy, & Williams, 1988; Murphy, Williams, & Dunning, 1990; Dunning, Murphy, Waddington, & Astrinakis, 2002); the globalization or international spread of sports (Maguire, 1999; 2000); sport and gender (Dunning, 1999, chap. 9); sport and race (Dunning, 1999, chap. 8); sport and

---

[4] It follows logically from the above that a society that grows poorer or where the state loses its violence and tax monopolies will experience decivilizing pressures and perhaps a decivilizing process of greater or lesser magnitude and duration.

"Figuring" Modern Sport

drugs, and the social aspects of sports injuries (Waddington, 2000). The range of sports covered has also increased and now includes soccer; rugby (Dunning & Sheard, 1979/2005); cricket (Malcolm, 2004); boxing (Sheard, 2004); baseball (Bloyce, 2004); gymnastics (Benn & Benn, 2004); motor sports (Twitchen, 2004); shooting (Smith, 2004); and Japanese martial arts (Kiku, 2004). Given the limited time available this evening, I shall only be able to deal with a couple of these topics; more particularly, the development of soccer and rugby and football hooliganism. I shall start with some autobiographical reminiscences.

In his Introduction to our 1986 book *Quest for Excitement*, Norbert Elias wrote:

> When we started on this work, the sociology of sport was still in its infancy. I well remember Eric Dunning discussing with me the question of whether sport, and particularly football, would be considered by the authorities to be a respectable subject of research in the social sciences and, in particular, for an MA thesis. I think we helped a little to make it that. (Elias & Dunning, 1986)

This appeared in 1986, some 26 or 27 years after I did my MA research under Norbert's supervision. Already, as an undergraduate, I had been attracted by his approach to sociology, but his open, supportive and non-authoritarian style of postgraduate supervision, and above all the discoveries that he helped me to make, confirmed my feeling that he was guiding me along the right lines[5].

---

[5] The Leicester Sociology Department in those days was very engaged. Central among the topics discussed by staff and students alike was

"Figuring" Modern Sport

My first task as an MA student was to construct a bibliography on the sociology of sport. The year, however, was 1959 and my literature search yielded only one item on sport in English that was unambiguously sociological: the late Gregory P. Stone's celebrated essay, "American sports: Play and dis-play"[6]. When I reported this to Norbert, he said: "Don't despair, Mr. Dunning." - British universities were much more formal in those days than they are today - "See if there are any histories of sport. Start with your favourite, football". So I did, and found that two or three histories of football had been written (Shearman, 1887; Magoun, 1938; Marples, 1954). I ordered them on inter-library loan and began to read them. As I did, a plan for my thesis began to form in my head. All these texts suggested that the modern football games - soccer, rugby, American, Gaelic and Australian rules - grew out of medieval British, Irish and Northern French antecedents which were considerably wilder and less regulated than are our modern forms. The texts also concurred in suggesting that the public schools and

---

Norbert Elias's position, which he referred to in those days as "developmental sociology". I remember in particular two heated but, as I saw them, "civilized" and constructive, debates between Norbert and John Goldthorpe and Norbert and Percy Cohen. Both Goldthorpe and Cohen used Popper's *The poverty of historicism* (1957) as the basis for an attack on Elias. I was inspired to read *The poverty of historicism* very carefully and somewhat later to write "In defence of developmental sociology: A critique of Popper's *Poverty of Historicism,* with special reference to the theory of Auguste Comte", *Amsterdams Sociologisch Tijdschrift,* 4 (3), 1977, 327-349: (reprinted in Dunning & Mennell, 2003).

[6] Greg Stone was one of the pioneers of the sociology of sport and played an active role in the early days of the International Committee for the Sociology of Sport (now the International Sociology of Sport Association).

"Figuring" Modern Sport

universities, especially Cambridge, played an important part in this development.

I speak German and had already glanced at Elias's two-volume work, *Über den Prozess der Zivilisation* (1939) — in English, *The Civilizing Process* - in the library as an undergraduate, so I described what I had read and said to him: "Dr. Elias, is this an example of a process of civilization of the kind you are concerned with in your book?" He replied: "Mr. Dunning, I don't know. You'll have to read my book and then I'll help you to devise a programme of research which will help you to find out". My research was broadly confirmatory of his theory, as was Ken Sheard's later research into rugby (1972), which was supervised by me. This research, together with my own MA thesis, is incorporated in our *Barbarians, Gentlemen and Players* (1979/2005). What we were basically testing is summarized in the following passage from the 2000 translation of *The Civilizing Process*, edited by Joop Goudsblom, Stephen Mennell and me. Elias wrote:

[In modern, "civilised", societies] ... belligerence and aggression find socially permitted expression in sporting contexts. And they are expressed especially in "spectating" (e.g., at boxing matches), in the imaginary identification with a small number of combatants to whom moderate and precisely regulated scope is granted for the release of such affects. And this living-out of affects in spectating or even in merely listening (e.g., to a radio commentary) is a particularly characteristic feature of civilized society. It partly determines the development of books and theatre, and decisively

"Figuring" Modern Sport

influences the role of the cinema in our world. This transformation of what manifested itself originally as an active, often aggressive expression of pleasure into the passive, more ordered pleasure of spectating (i.e., the mere pleasure of the eye) is already initiated in education, in the conditioning precepts for young people .... It is highly characteristic of civilized people that they are denied by socially instilled self-controls from spontaneously touching what they desire, love or hate. (Elias, 2000, p. 170)

A taboo on touching for all players except the goalkeeper has, of course, become the major distinguishing characteristic of the soccer form of football. Let me begin to explore how and why. The process I am about to describe is the subject of Ken Sheard's and my recently re-issued *Barbarians, Gentlemen and Players* (1979/2005). I shall also incorporate into this part of my lecture references to some of the work of Graham Curry (2001), another PhD student supervised by me.

As I hinted earlier, the modern forms of football are descended from a type of medieval/early modern folk games that was played according to local custom, rather than written rules that have been bureaucratically established by a national or international ruling body. These games were played across open country or through the streets of towns, rather than in a specifically designated stadium or field and on a specifically marked out playing area or pitch. They were played, not between teams in our modern sense, but between the representatives of occupational groups, groups such as bachelors versus married men, or groups representing sections of towns.

13

"Figuring" Modern Sport

No attempt was made to equalize numbers between the contending sides. Hands as well as feet and sometimes sticks could be used to control and propel the ball, and each side had to transport the ball to what was decreed by custom as their goal.

The evidence for this type of games consists of two main sources: prohibitions by state and local authorities, and descriptions of cognate folk games such as Cornish "hurling" and Welsh "knappan". I have chosen to illustrate such games and the furore they aroused by an account from Chester, which Morris Marples dates from 1533 and Percy Young from 1539. The account was written by Archdeacon Robert Rogers, who died in 1595, in an essay which he entitled: "Of the laudable exercises yearely used within the cittie of Chester". I have not chosen this extract simply because I am lecturing in Chester. It is also sociologically very interesting, among other reasons because it is an early and apparently successful example of getting people to accept what some sociologists would call a "functional substitute" or "functional alternative" (Merton, 1949) for an activity which the authorities wanted to ban. Archdeacon Rogers's account reads:

Mem: That whereas the companye and corporation of shoemakers

within the cittie of Chester, did yearely, time out of memory of

man, upon Tewsday, or otherwise *Gotesdesse* day afternoon, at the

cross upon the Rood Dee, before the mayor of the said cittie, offer

unto the company of drapers of the said cittie, a ball of leather,

called a foote-ball, of the value of 3s. and 4d. or thereabout: and by

reason of great strife which did arise among the younge persons of

"Figuring" Modern Sport

the same cittie (while diverse parties were taken with force and stronge handes to bring the said ball to one of these three houses, that is to say, to the mayor's house, or any one of the two sheriffes' houses of the time being), much harme was done, some in the great thronge falling into a trance, some having their bodies bruised and crushed; some their arms, heades or legges broken, and some otherwise maimed, or in peril of life; to avoid the said inconveniences, and also to forme and converte the said homage to a better use; it was thought good by the mayor of the said cittie, and the rest of the common council, to exchange of the said foote-ball as followeth: that in place thereof there be offered by the shoemakers to the drapers six gleaves of silver[7], the which gleaves they appointed to be rewards unto such men as would come, and the same day and place, passe and overcome on foote all others ....

(cited in Young, 1968, pp. 17-18)

The mayor of Chester at the time was Henry Gee and the "functional alternative" to the "hooligan" game of football that he instituted was a foot race. According to Marples (1954, p. 46), Mayor Gee also inaugurated a horse-race - said to have been the origin of the present-day Chester races - and offered prizes for shooting. In other words, in this way what were called in another then-contemporary

---

[7] A "gleave" was an arrow.

15

"Figuring" Modern Sport

account "three of the most commendable exercises and practices of war-like feates" were instituted as annual events in Chester; namely running, riding and shooting. Presumably, even though he is known to have played football himself in his youth, King Henry VIII would have been pleased! However, as is suggested by the extract from Elias that I quoted earlier, one of the major thrusts in the development of modern sports has been to make them less directly war-like than their antecedents. The public schools and universities played an important role in this "process of civilization". It is to that issue that I shall now turn.

The folk forms of football were under attack from the authorities from at least 1314 when, along with a number of other leisure activities, they were banned in the name of Edward II on the grounds that they were a threat to public order and national military preparedness, because they took people away from archery practice (Dunning, 1999). However, as is nowadays proving to be the case with regard to *spectator* hooliganism, custom was stronger than the law in relation to these player forms and it was not until the early nineteenth century that the folk forms of football began, not to disappear altogether, but to be culturally marginalized (Dunning & Sheard, 1979/2005, pp. 21-39).

In the late eighteenth and early nineteenth centuries, forms of football continued to be played by two main groups: by local teams associated mainly with pubs (Harvey, 2001) and by boys in the leading public schools. Pub matches tended to be played for stake money or served as foci for gambling. As Elias (in Elias & Dunning, 1986) has shown in relation to boxing and cricket, the addition of a money element was conducive to a degree of regularization, and matches began for the first time to be played between sides, not of fixed but of equal numbers,

"Figuring" Modern Sport

for example, three a side, six a side, nine a side, eleven a side, fifteen a side or twenty a side. However, as I said earlier, it was in the public schools and universities - particularly Cambridge - that the modern forms of football began to develop. Both a civilizing process and a related non-violent process of status competition were at work in this connection. Let me elaborate on this.

Initially formed as charitable institutions for the education of poor boys, the public schools were transformed in the eighteenth and early nineteenth centuries into boarding schools for the upper and upper middle classes. At least two consequences followed from this upper and upper middle class takeover: the first was that the class discrepancy between masters and pupils, inherent in a type of school where middle class teachers were attempting to educate boys who mostly came from higher social strata than themselves, meant that the masters were unable to prevent the emergence of a form of self-rule by the boys: the prefect-fagging system. The second was that this power and status discrepancy led to chronic discipline problems in the schools, some of them even taking the form of open rebellion (Dunning & Sheard, 1979/2005; Dunning, 1999).

Sports, including football, were one of the means employed by masters in an attempt to cope with these discipline problems. However, the public school forms of football were at first as wild and unregulated as the folk forms in the wider society. Hence their educational use was limited. In fact, in the public schools, the wildness of folk football was if anything reinforced. At each school, the game came to be one of the means through which older boys asserted dominance over their juniors. One of the customary duties that developed for the "fags" was what they called "fagging out" at football. This meant that fags, the junior boys, were compelled by their seniors to play

"Figuring" Modern Sport

and restricted for the most part to the role of "keeping goal". That is, they were ranged en masse along the base lines. For example, we are told that, at Westminster in the early nineteenth century, "the small boys, the duffers and the funk-sticks were the goalkeepers, twelve or fifteen at each end". "Douling", the name they gave to football at Shrewsbury, was the same as they used for "fagging". It is derived, I understand, from the Greek word for "slave". At Winchester in the early nineteenth century, fags, one at either end, were even used instead of goal-posts, the ball having to be kicked between their outstretched legs to score. Lines of fags were also used as a means of boundary demarcation (Dunning & Sheard, 1979/2005).

Handling the ball as well as kicking was allowed at *all* the public schools at this stage. All forms of public school football at this stage were also rough. For example, in Charterhouse "field football", we hear that "there were a good many broken shins, for most of the fellows had iron tips to their very strong shoes and some freely boasted of giving more than they took"! Iron-tipped boots were also used at Rugby, where they called them "navvies". According to an Old Rugbeian reminiscing in the 1920s, navvies had "a thick sole, the profile of which at the toe much resembled the ram of an ironclad". (Dunning & Sheard, 1979/2005; Dunning, 1999).

Written rules of football were first produced at Rugby in 1845. Rugby, under Thomas Arnold, was also the first public school where effective reform of the prefect-fagging system was achieved. Both were "civilizing" developments: reform of the prefect-fagging system because it reduced the arbitrary power of older in relation to younger boys; the codification and regularization of football because these processes were aimed at abolishing the use of "navvies" and at reducing the violence of practices such as "shinning" and "hacking over". There is

"Figuring" Modern Sport

also reason to believe that reform of the prefect-fagging system was a precondition for the reform of football at the school.

The second public school to commit its football rules to writing was Eton in 1847. These were in many ways diametrically opposite to their counterparts at Rugby, where carrying the ball and scoring by kicking it above H-shaped goalposts were legislated for in the rules of 1845. One of the 1847 Eton rules, for example, reads: "Hands may only be used to stop the ball, or touch it when behind. The ball must not be carried, thrown or struck by the hand". These rules can thus be seen as legislating for an embryonic form of "soccer" (Dunning, 1999).

Why should the boys at Eton have wanted to produce such a game? Under Arnold, the fame of Rugby School had begun to spread and, with it, the fame of their football. The Rugby boys, encouraged by their staff, were, it seems reasonable to suppose, seeking to draw attention to themselves by developing a distinctive game. However, it would seem similarly not unlikely that, by developing a form of football which was equally distinctive, but in key respects diametrically opposite to the game at Rugby, the Etonians were deliberately attempting to put the "upstart" Rugbeians in their place. As I mentioned earlier, status competition between upper class and rising middle class groups, as Elias (1939/2000) showed, has played an important part in the civilizing processes of Europe. More particularly, in "phases of colonization", members of the latter would adopt the manners and standards of the former, leading these upper class groups in "phases of repulsion" to develop, as means of status demarcation and exclusion, more refined standards involving the imposition of a demand for the exercise of even greater self-control. The hands are among the most important bodily implements of humans and, by placing a near absolute

19

"Figuring" Modern Sport

taboo on their use in a game, the Etonians were demanding that players should learn to exercise self-control of a high order. In a soccer-playing society today, in which children learn to kick the ball and not to use their hands from a young age, this might not seem like a very difficult demand. However, when it was first introduced, it must have been equivalent to being required to balance peas on the back of one's fork. Indeed, we hear that, when Etonians and others first tried to introduce the non-handling game to members of the working class, the latter were required to play holding a shilling and were allowed to keep it if they succeeded in not using their hands!

Support for the status-competition hypothesis comes from the fact that Eton-Rugby rivalry was a major axis of tension in football relations at Cambridge in the mid-nineteenth century (Dunning, 1999). For example, we hear that, at Trinity College in 1848, "the Eton men howled at the Rugby men for handling the ball". They evidently regarded it as vulgar. Compromise football rules were produced at Cambridge somewhere between 1837 and 1842, in 1846, 1848, in about 1856 and in 1863. Trinity Old Etonians were predominant in the production of most of these rules, but especially those of 1863 (Curry, 2001). These were based largely on the Eton Field Game and formed the central basis on which the first rules of the Football Association were produced, also in 1863.

Throughout the 1850s and 1860s, rugby spread more widely and more quickly than soccer. However, this changed in 1871-72, with the introduction of the FA Cup. This enhanced the popularity of soccer and it soon became predominantly working class and, at its highest levels, professional. This status reversal of soccer and rugby led the Master of an Oxbridge College in the 1890s famously to describe soccer as "a game for gentlemen played by hooligans" and rugby as "a game for hooligans played by

"Figuring" Modern Sport

gentlemen". It is to the figurational research into football hooliganism and why such deviant behaviour has become so firmly entrenched in soccer that I shall finally turn my attention.

The figurational approach to football hooliganism does not constitute a "super theory" that explains everything about the phenomenon. It is offered only as a beginning on which to build. Its distinctive features are that it is based on a synthesis of psychology, sociology and history, and that it involves an exploration of the meanings of hooligan behaviour to the hooligans themselves. In this last regard, analysis of a range of hooligan statements made over a period of more than 30 years revealed that, for the (mainly) young men involved, football hooligan fighting is basically about masculinity, territorial struggle and excitement. For them, fighting is a central source of meaning, status or "reputation", and pleasurable emotional arousal. They speak of the respect among their peers that they hope their hooligan involvements will bring, and of "battle excitement", "the adrenaline racing", and of "aggro" as almost erotically arousing. Indeed, Jay Allan, a leading member of "the Aberdeen Casuals", a Scottish football hooligan "firm" in the 1980s, wrote of fighting at football as even more pleasurable than sex (1989). American author Bill Buford, who travelled with English football hooligans in the 1980s, described it in the book he wrote about them thus: "... violence is one of the most intensely lived experiences and, for those capable of giving themselves over to it, one of the most intense pleasures .... Crowd violence was their drug" (1991, p. 201).

Table I (overleaf) summarizes what is known about the occupational class of employed English football hooligans and trends in this regard between 1968 and 1987. Research on the social class of football hooligans in Scotland

"Figuring" Modern Sport

(Harper, 1990), Belgium (Limbergen & Walgrave, 1988), the Netherlands (Brug, 1986) and Italy (Roversi, 1992) suggests that hooligans in other countries tend to come from social backgrounds similar to those of their English counterparts.

Table I[8]

Trends in the Occupational Class of Employed English Football Hooligans, 1968-1987[9]

Occupational Class	Harrington, 1968		Stuttard/Dunning et al, 1985		Armstrong, 1987[10]	
	Number	%	Number	%	Number	%
Professional	2	0.5[11]			3	2.1
Intermediate			8	5.7	7	4.9
Skilled Non-Manual	19	4.9	2	1.42	24	16.8
Skilled Manual	50	12.9[12]	34	24.1	67	46.8
Semi-Skilled	112	28.8	10	7.0	14	9.8
Unskilled	206	52.9	25	17.7[13]	28	19.6

The fact that violent spectator disorder occurs more frequently in conjunction with soccer than any other sport would thus appear to be partly a function of the social composition of its crowds. Soccer is the world's most popular team sport and, worldwide, a majority of its spectators tend to be male and to come from the lower

---

[8] Source: Dunning, Murphy, Waddington, & Astrinakis (2002, p. 19)

[9] Figures exclude those for schoolboys, apprentices, the unemployed and those with occupations unclassifiable in terms of the Registrar General's scheme.

[10] Armstrong's 1987 data published in Armstrong (1998).

[11] Professional and intermediate classified together.

[12] Harrington uses different categories.

[13] 32 (22.7%) of our ICF sample were unemployed at the time and 30 (21.2%) were unclassifiable using the Registrar General's categories. 12 of the latter earned a living as ticket touts and 8 were members of the armed forces.

"Figuring" Modern Sport

reaches of the social scale; that is, from social backgrounds where norms tend to legitimate a higher incidence of overt aggressiveness and violence in everyday social relations than tends to be the case among the middle and upper classes[14]. More particularly, lower class males tend to develop a violent and aggressive habitus and mode of presenting themselves to the world. This involves a complex of learned traits which seem fundamentally to derive inter alia from:

1. A pattern of early socialization characterized by ready resort to violence by parents and siblings; and
2. Adolescent socialization on the streets in the company of age peers, i.e. in adolescent "gangs" (Dunning, Murphy, & Williams, 1988).

In these figurations, because ability and willingness to fight are criteria for membership of and prestige within the group - i.e., for the status of these males in their own and others' eyes as "men" - they learn to associate adrenaline arousal in fight situations with warm, rewarding and hence pleasurable feelings, rather than with the guilt and anxiety that tend to surround the performance and witnessing of "real" (as opposed to "mimetic") violence in the wider society.

This kind of violent habitus tends to be reinforced to the extent that such males live and work in figurations characterized by high levels of gender and age-group segregation. That is because of the relative absence in such figurations of "softening" pressure from females and older men. Furthermore, in most societies, groups lower down the social scale are less likely to be highly individualized and more likely readily to form intense "we-group" bonds and identifications (Elias, 1978, pp. 134-148), which involve

---

[14] Members of these higher groups are more liable to conform in public (though not necessarily in private) with official standards.

"Figuring" Modern Sport

an equally intense hostility towards "outsiders" (Elias & Scotson, 1994) than is the case among the more powerful, more cosmopolitan, more self-steering and usually more inhibited groups who stand above them. At a soccer match, of course, the outsiders are the opposing team and its supporters and, in some cases, the match officials. Soccer tends to be chosen by these groups as a context in which to fight because it, too, is about masculinity, territorial struggle and excitement. Given a widespread pattern of travel to away matches, the game also regularly provides a set of ready-made opponents with whom to fight. Moreover, large crowds form a context where it is possible to behave violently and in other deviant ways with a relatively good chance of escaping detection and arrest.

Having said this, it would be wrong to view soccer hooliganism as always and everywhere a function solely or mainly of class. As a basis for further research, it is reasonable to hypothesize that the problem is contoured and fuelled, ceteris paribus, by what one might call the major "fault-lines" of particular countries. In England, that means class and regional differences and inequalities; in Scotland and Northern Ireland, religious sectarianism; in Spain, the partly language-based sub-nationalisms of the Catalans, Castilians and Basques; in Italy, city-based particularism and perhaps the division between North and South as expressed in the formation of the "Northern League"; and in Germany, relations between the generations (Heitmeyer & Peter, 1988; Elias, 1996) and those between East and West. Religious, sub-national, city-based, regional and generation-based fault-lines may draw into football and football hooliganism more people from higher up the social scale than tends to be the case in England. Arguably, however, a shared characteristic of all these fault-lines - and, of course, each can overlap and

"Figuring" Modern Sport

interact with others in a variety of complex ways - is that they correspond to what Elias (Elias & Scotson, 1994) called "established-outsider figurations", that is, social formations involving intense "we-group" bonds ("us") and correspondingly intense antagonisms towards "outsiders" or "they-groups" ("them").

The association of hooliganism with soccer is also partly a function of the greater world-wide media exposure that the game receives. Other sports do not get as much media coverage; accordingly, such violence as accompanies them is not so publicly apparent. The media also tend to generate myths and these, too, contribute to public perceptions. For example, in the years from the late 1920s to the mid-1960s, the occurrence of soccer hooliganism in Central and South America, continental Europe (especially the Latin countries), Scotland, Wales and Northern Ireland was regularly reported in the English press, together with statements to the effect that such behaviour "couldn't happen in England". However, unruly behaviour had been rife at English soccer matches before the First World War and had never died out completely (Dunning, Murphy, & Williams, 1988, pp. 32-90). The 1960s were also the period in which the present-day forms of English football hooliganism and media coverage, which sometimes approached the level of a moral panic, started to emerge.

References

Allan, J. (1989). *Bloody Casual: Diary of a football hooligan.* [Gartochan]: Famedram.

Armstrong, G. (1998). *Football hooligans: Knowing the score.* Oxford: Berg.

"Figuring" Modern Sport

Benn, T., & Benn, B. (2004). After Olga: Developments in women's artistic gymnastics following the 1972 'Olga Korbut phenomenon'. In E. Dunning, D. Malcolm, & I. Waddington (Eds.), *Sport histories: Figurational studies of the development of modern sports* (pp. 172-190). London: Routledge.

Bloyce, D. (2004). Baseball: Myths and modernization. In E. Dunning, D. Malcolm, & I. Waddington (Eds.), *Sport histories: Figurational studies of the development of modern sports* (pp. 88-103). London: Routledge.

Brug, H. H. van der (1986). *Voetbalvandalisme.* Haarlem: De Vrieseborch.

Buford, B. (1991). *Among the thugs.* London: Secker & Warburg.

Curry, G. (2001). *Football: A study in diffusion.* Unpublished doctoral dissertation, University of Leicester.

Dunning, E. (1961). *Early stages in the development of football as an organized game: An account of some of the sociological problems in the development of a game.* Unpublished master's thesis, University of Leicester.

Dunning, E. (1977). In defence of developmental sociology: a critique of Popper's *Poverty of Historicism,* with special

"Figuring" Modern Sport

reference to the theory of Auguste Comte. *Amsterdams Sociologisch Tijdschrift, 4* (3), 327-349.

Dunning, E. (1999). *Sport matters: Sociological studies of sport, violence and civilization.* London: Routledge.

Dunning, E., Malcolm, D., & Waddington, I. (Eds.). (2004). *Sport histories: Figurational studies of the development of modern sports.* London: Routledge.

Dunning, E., & Mennell, S. (Eds.). (2003). *Norbert Elias.* (Vols. 1-4). London: Sage.

Dunning, E., Murphy, P., Waddington, I., & Astrinakis, A. (Eds.). (2002). *Fighting fans: Football hooliganism as a world phenomenon.* Dublin: University College Dublin Press.

Dunning, E., Murphy, P., & Williams, J. (1988). *The roots of football hooliganism: An historical and sociological study.* London: Routledge.

Dunning, E., & Sheard, K. (1979). *Barbarians, gentlemen and players: A sociological study of the development of rugby football.* Oxford: Martin Robertson.

Reprinted, with a new appendix: (2005). London: Routledge.

Durkheim, E. (1938). *The rules of sociological method* (S. A. Solovay & T. H. Mueller, Trans.; G. E. G. Catlin, Ed.).

"Figuring" Modern Sport

(8th ed.). Glencoe, IL: Free Press. (Original work published 1895).

Durkheim, E. (1964). *The division of labour in society* (G. Simpson, Trans.). Glencoe, IL: Free Press. (Original work published 1893; this translation originally published 1933).

Elias, N. (1978). *What is sociology?* (S. Mennell & G. Morrissey, Trans.). London: Hutchinson. (Original work published 1970).

Elias, N. (1996). *The Germans: power struggles and the development of habitus in the nineteenth and twentieth centuries* (M. Schröter, Ed.; E Dunning & S Mennell, Trans.). Cambridge: Polity Press. (Original work published 1989).

Elias, N. (2000). *The civilizing process: sociogenetic and psychogenetic investigations, with some notes and corrections by the author* (E. Dunning, J. Goudsblom, & S. Mennell, Eds.; E. Jephcott, Trans.). (Rev. integrated ed.). Oxford: Blackwell. (Original work published 1939).

Elias, N., & Dunning, E. (1986). *Quest for excitement: Sport and leisure in the civilizing process.* Oxford: Blackwell.

"Figuring" Modern Sport

Elias, N., & Scotson, J. (1994). *The established and the outsiders: A sociological enquiry into community problems.* (2nd ed.). London: Sage. (Original work published 1965).

Goudsblom, J. (1992). *Fire and civilization.* London: Allen Lane.

Harper, C. (1990). *A study of football crowd behaviour: 1989-90.* Edinburgh: Lothian and Borders Police.

Harrington, J. A. (1968). *Soccer hooliganism: a preliminary report to Mr. Denis Howell, Minister of Sport, by a Birmingham research group.* Bristol: John Wright.

Harvey, A. (2001). 'An epoch in the annals of national sport': Football in Sheffield and the creation of modern soccer and rugby. *The International Journal of the History of Sport, 18* (4), 53-87.

Heitmeyer, W., & Peter, J.-I. (1988). *Jugendliche Fussballfans: Soziale und politische Orientierungen, Gesellschaftsformen, Gewalt.* Weinheim: Juventa-Verlag.

Kiku, K. (2004). The development of sport in Japan: Martial arts and baseball. In E. Dunning, D. Malcolm, & I. Waddington (Eds.), *Sport histories: Figurational studies of the development of modern sports* (pp. 153-171). London: Routledge.

"Figuring" Modern Sport

Limbergen, K. van, & Walgrave, L. (1988). *Sides, fans en hooligans: Voetbalvandalisme: Feiten, achtergronden en aanpak.* Leuven: Acco.

Magoun, F. P. (1938). *History of football from the beginnings to 1871.* Bochum-Langendreer : H. Pöppinghaus.

Maguire, J. (1999). *Global sport: Identities, societies, civilizations.* Cambridge: Polity Press.

Maguire, J. (2000). Sport and globalization. In J. Coakley & E. Dunning. (Eds.). *Handbook of sports studies* (pp. 356-369). London: Sage.

Maguire, J., & Young, K. (Eds.). (2002). *Theory, sport & society.* Amsterdam: JAI.

Malcolm, D. (2004). Cricket: Civilizing and de-civilizing processes in the imperial game. In E. Dunning, D. Malcolm, & I. Waddington (Eds.), *Sport histories: Figurational studies of the development of modern sports* (pp. 71-87). London: Routledge.

Marples, M. (1954). *A history of football.* London: Secker & Warburg.

Mennell, S. (1985). *All manners of food: Eating and taste in England and France from the Middle Ages to the present.* Oxford: Blackwell.

"Figuring" Modern Sport

Merton, R. K. (1949). *Social theory and social structure: Toward the codification of theory and research.* Glencoe, IL: Free Press.

Murphy, P., Williams, J., & Dunning, E. (1990). *Football on trial: Spectator violence and development in the football world.* London: Routledge.

Popper, K. R. (1957). *The poverty of historicism.* London: Routledge and Kegan Paul.

Roversi, A. (1992). *Calcio, tifo e violenza : Il teppismo calcistico in Italia.* Bologna: Il Mulino.

Sheard, K. (1972). *Rugby football: A study in developmental sociology.* Unpublished master's thesis, University of Leicester.

Sheard, K. (2004). Boxing in the Western civilizing process. In E. Dunning, D. Malcolm, & I. Waddington (Eds.), *Sport histories: Figurational studies of the development of modern sports* (pp. 15-30). London: Routledge.

Shearman, M. (1887). *Athletics and football.* London: Longmans, Green.

Smith, S. (2004). Clay shooting: Civilization in the line of fire. In E. Dunning, D. Malcolm, & I. Waddington (Eds.), *Sport histories: Figurational studies of the*

"Figuring" Modern Sport

development of modern sports (pp. 137-152). London: Routledge.

Stone, G. P. (1955). American sports: Play and dis-play. *Chicago Review, 9,* 83-100.

Stuttard, I. (Producer). (1985). *Hooligan* [Television broadcast]. London: Thames Television.

Twitchen, A. (2004). The influence of state-formation processes on the early development of motor racing. In E. Dunning, D. Malcolm, & I. Waddington (Eds.), *Sport histories: Figurational studies of the development of modern sports* (pp. 121-136). London: Routledge.

Waddington, I. (2000). *Sport, health and drugs: A critical sociological perspective.* London: Spon.

Young, P. M. (1968). *A history of British football.* London: Stanley Paul.